Making

Martingale®
& C O M P A N Y

Beautiful Jewelry

Tone Rørseth

Making Beautiful Jewelry
Tone Rørseth
©2007 N. W. Damm & Søn AS, Oslo, Norway
First printing: 2007
Photography: Erika Lidén
Stylist: Tone Rørseth
First published in the United States in 2008 by
Martingale & Company®
20205 144th Ave. NE
Woodinville, WA 98072-8478 USA
www.martingale-pub.com

Martingale®
& C O M P A N Y

Cover and Interior Design: Stan Green
Technical Editing: Robin Strobel
Translation: Carol Huebscher Rhoades

Library of Congress Cataloging-in-Publication Data
Library of Congress Control Number: 2008027483

ISBN: 978-1-56477-896-3

Printed in China
13 12 11 10 09 08   8 7 6 5 4 3 2 1

MISSION STATEMENT
Dedicated to providing quality products and service to inspire creativity.

Contents

Introduction

Welcome to the exciting world of jewelry making!

Whether you're taking your first steps toward making your own jewelry or you're an experienced enthusiast, I hope this book will inspire you to play with and enjoy the jewelry you can create with beads, wire, and pretty little accents. With this in mind, I have designed jewelry that is easy to make, fun to wear, and that won't cost the earth.

The jewelry in this book is first and foremost intended to provide inspiration and a starting point for your own creativity. I hope you'll be inspired to make your jewelry with colors and materials different from mine. Jewelry and clothing reveal something about who you are or who you want to be on a particular day or occasion. You'll gain a sense of freedom by taking chances and trying out new decorative expressions.

My starting point when choosing materials is to look around the house. Button collections, beads from broken chains, flea market finds, loose pendants, little treasures from nature, and even Grandmother's workbasket can offer a wealth

of small objects. When I design jewelry, my goals are to make something beautiful, to have a creative and enjoyable hobby, and to bring my creativity into other aspects of everyday life.

After many years of experimentation, I've discovered that a super idea isn't always so wonderful once I've actually tried it. How many wires should I form and bend, how tightly should copper wire be crocheted, and how many colors should be combined? My second attempt is often much better than the first. If this is the first time you've made jewelry, think of it as a game and don't give up if initially it doesn't go as well as you expected. You may feel a little overwhelmed at first, but that's often how the creative process works. Keep playing and building your skills and let the materials guide you.

Have fun!

Tools and Materials

You can find materials and tools for making jewelry in hobby and bead shops as well as through mail order and the Internet. To begin with, you need three tools: round-nose pliers, flat-nose pliers, and side- or flush-cutting wire cutters. Depending on what type of jewelry you want to make, you will probably need some other tools, but these will get you started.

Jewelry wire in various materials, colors, and diameters (gauges) is an important basic. Copper wire is inexpensive and good for practicing and experimenting. Brass and copper wires come in many terrific colors. Silver- and gold-colored copper wire, some of which is plastic-coated, is available in rolls. If you want to work with true silver and gold wire, it is sold in many bead shops, in hobby shops, and through mail order and the Internet.

In the United States, the diameter of the wire is indicated in gauges. The smaller the gauge, the thicker the wire. For many of the projects in this book, I've used 20-gauge wire because it's strong and durable. Thinner 24-gauge wire is easier to work with, and very thin 28-gauge wire is good for crochet and for wrapping around stones and beads.

There are many small items you can buy to make jewelry making easier. Some of the practical items I've used in this book are shown on the facing page.

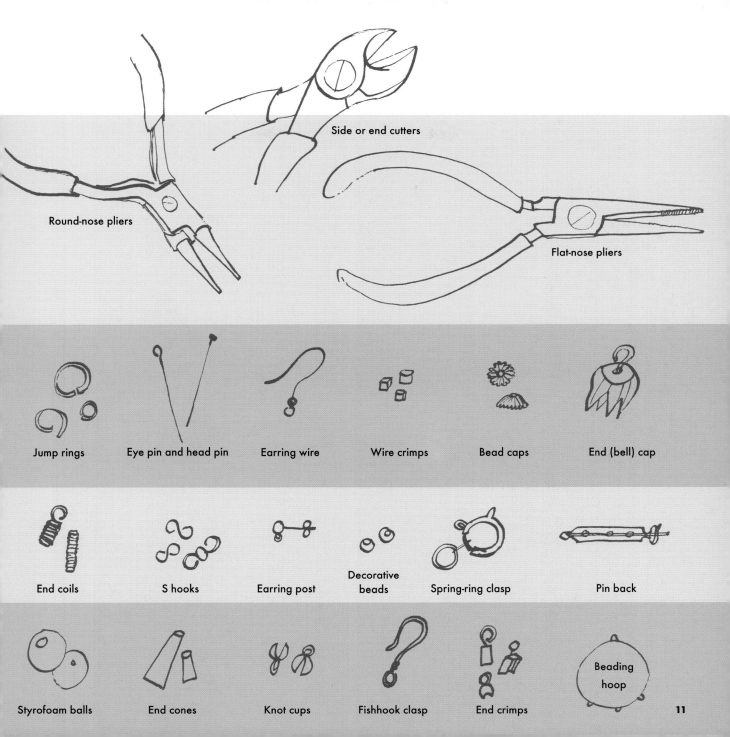

Side or end cutters

Round-nose pliers

Flat-nose pliers

Jump rings

Eye pin and head pin

Earring wire

Wire crimps

Bead caps

End (bell) cap

End coils

S hooks

Earring post

Decorative beads

Spring-ring clasp

Pin back

Styrofoam balls

End cones

Knot cups

Fishhook clasp

End crimps

Beading hoop

11

Jewelry with Buttons, Coins, and Cork Beads

Look for old buttons in the sewing basket. Maybe you have some old or foreign coins. Combine them with cork, glass, rubber, and mother-of-pearl discs, and tie them all on a cord.

Materials:
Waxed jewelry cord
Buttons, charms, coins, mother-of-pearl discs
Assorted beads

Use waxed jewelry cord because it is easy to knot and comes in many colors. The knots will hold well, although they can be difficult to untie if that becomes necessary.

For the necklace, cut a cord about one yard long. Randomly tie your choice of various buttons, charms, and beads to the cord. Your items and colors will be different than mine. I livened up my selection with bright green charms and mother-of-pearl discs that shift colors. You can wear the necklace as a lariat or wrap it twice around your neck. It also makes a nice bracelet if you wrap it four or five times around your wrist.

For a simple bracelet, cut 18" of waxed jewelry cord. Knot most of the beads and buttons at the center of the cord. Tie a bow to fasten it around your wrist.

Earrings with Beads, Threads, and Chains

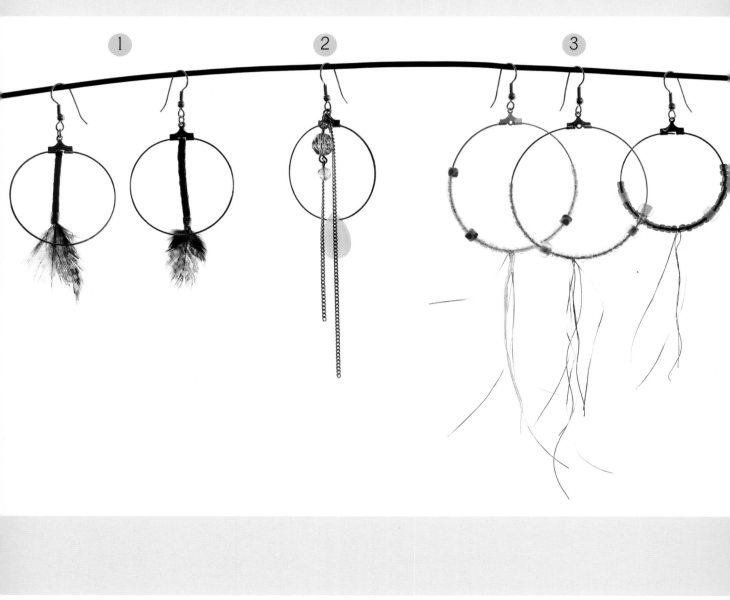

It's rewarding to make your own earrings, because you just have to buy earring wires and then embellish them with hoops, large and small beads, threads, feathers, or other accents.

Style 1

For each earring, cut a 1¼" to 1½" piece of satin cord. Glue and crimp a feather and a cord tip without an eye to one end. Glue and crimp a cord tip with an eye to the other end. When the glue is dry, attach the cord and a beading hoop to the base of an earring wire.

Style 2

For each earring, thread a large stone or bead on a beading hoop. Thread a small bead on a head pin. Trim the excess wire and form a loop. Thread a medium bead on an eye pin, trim, make a loop, and join to the small bead. Hang the beads, the beading hoop, and two different lengths of chain on an earring wire.

Style 3

For each earring, thread small beads on a beading hoop. Spark up the selection with an occasional bead in another color or size. Cut one to two strands each of metallic and sewing thread, about 4" to 5" long. Tie the threads at the center of the beads. Tie a double knot to make sure the threads will hold. Attach the hoop to an earring wire.

Pendant Jewelry

An assortment of balls and beads, old pieces of brooches, and bits of broken jewelry make great materials for a pendant necklace. Maybe you've inherited some pearls or other simple pieces of jewelry that you can recycle in a lovely new necklace. For this piece, you want the opposite of simplicity—the more the better. A chain with links at least 4 mm in diameter makes it easy to attach all the elements. To balance the many different components of the necklace, I've used a simple color scheme.

Necklace

Use the jump ring to attach the 4¼" chain to the midpoint of the 16" chain. Arrange the beads and pieces in the order you want them on the necklace. Thread each piece with a head pin. Trim the excess wire and form a loop.

Attach all the pieces to the chain. To make everything lie nicely around your neck, be careful to attach the pieces to the same side of the chain. Attach the toggle clasp to the ends of the necklace.

Bracelet

Use the same technique and a lobster-claw or toggle clasp to make a bracelet. Wrists can vary in size, so measure before cutting the chain.

Ring

Use the wire for the center pin. Make a little eye loop on one end of the wire and attach it to one end of the chain. Thread one to three small beads on the wire, trim the excess, and make a small eye loop, attaching it to the other end of the chain.

Materials for Necklace:
One 24-gauge jump ring
4¼" of large-link chain
16" of large-link chain
Assorted beads, stones, balls,
     medallions, and charms
Head pins
Toggle clasp

Materials for Bracelet:
Assorted beads, stones, balls,
     medallions, and charms
8" of large-link chain
Head pins
Lobster-claw or spring-ring clasp

Materials for Ring:
1" of 22-gauge wire
3 small beads
1½" of approximately 2 mm-
     diameter chain

This bracelet has a warm-tone color scheme.

Plastic Jewelry

Plastic offers lots of new and fun possibilities. If you don't have thick, pliable plastic on hand, you can substitute plastic pockets. It's fun to make bracelets with photos or paper cutouts. Use pictures of a loved one, a pet, or something that you treasure.

Materials for Bracelet:
3½" x 8" piece of clear, smooth plastic
1½" x 7½" photo or paper cutout
Snap
Hand-sewing needle and thread
Sewing machine

Bracelet

Fold the plastic in half so it measures 1¾" x 8". Thread your sewing machine with one color on the top and a different color in the bobbin. Zigzag stitch close to the edge around three sides of the plastic pocket, leaving one short side open. Place a photo or paper cutout in the plastic pocket. For a reversible bracelet, put two pictures wrong sides together. Zigzag stitch the short side closed. Sew one part of the snap to the end of the bracelet on the right side; sew the other part to the other end of the bracelet on the wrong side. If you plan to change the picture often, leave the end open and sew the snap to only one layer of plastic.

Necklace

Cut the plastic in half so the two pieces measure 1½" x 2¼". Hold the pieces together and zigzag stitch close to the edge around three sides, leaving the long top edge unsewn. Cut the threads, leaving 2" tails. Tie four to five small beads to each thread (tie a knot around each bead, with a double knot around the last bead). Trim two pictures so they will fit, and place them wrong sides together in the plastic pocket.

Cut two lengths of waxed jewelry cord. The length of the strands can vary. I cut one strand 19" and the other 16". Tie a spring-ring clasp to one end of one cord and a jump ring to one end of the other cord. Tie some colorful plastic beads here and there, being careful to place a bead about 8" from the clasp on each cord to provide a stopper for the pocket.

Punch a small hole at each top corner of the pocket. Insert a jump ring in each hole and attach to the jewelry cord just above the beads that are 8" from the clasp.

Materials for Necklace:

2¼" x 3" piece of smooth, clear plastic
Plastic beads
2 photos or paper cutouts
Waxed jewelry cord
Spring-ring clasp
Three 4 mm jump rings
Sewing machine

Ring

Use a metal ring that has holes in the top (available at bead shops or online). Thread the needle, and beginning with one bead at the center of the ring, make a double knot and attach it to the top of the perforated screen so that there is 3" of thread hanging down on one end. String the beads on the other end of the thread, weaving through the screen and the beads and building the beads around the first one in a little pile. Make sure that the thread holds the beads securely. Finish by bringing the thread to the back of the base. Tie the thread ends together, trim, and put a drop of glue on the knot so that it holds firmly.

Materials for Ring:

Metal ring with perforated beading screen
Beading needle
12" of beading thread or fishing line
3 to 4 mm plastic beads
Quick-drying glue

Plastic-Coated Wire Necklace and Earrings

This design features various lengths that remind me of the planets in orbit around the sun. The necklaces are made with plastic-coated beading wire that is available in a variety of colors. Decorate the wires with a crocheted ball or small pearls and beads. This type of wire also works well as long, straight drops for earrings.

Necklace

Cut a piece of beading wire the shortest length you'd like around the neck. The example was cut 14¾". Cut four lengths total, making each succeeding wire ¾" longer than the last. You can use each wire length as is, glue on some freshwater pearls, or attach a crocheted wire ball. Bring one end of the beading wires together, add a drop of glue, and insert the ends into an end coil. Repeat at the opposite end. Tighten the end coils and attach a spring-ring clasp and jump ring.

Crocheted Ball Embellishment

With the 28-gauge wire, chain 2 to 3 stitches. Make a slip stitch into the first chain to join in the round. Work several rounds of single crochet, making a little plate by increasing stitches in each round until you have 17 stitches. Decrease at the same rate as you increased until you are back to the original number of stitches. Insert a freshwater pearl in the center of the ball. Pull the tail of wire through the last stitch and cut. Shape the piece into a mini ball. Thread the shortest length of beading wire through the top of the ball. Thread the remaining wires in order of length, finishing with the longest wire on the bottom. It is important that the strands stay in the same order from the ball to the end coils.

Earrings

For each earring, cut four 3¼"-long pieces of plastic-coated wire. Hold the strands together and glue them into an end coil. Let dry completely, and then attach them to an earring post.

Materials:

Plastic-coated .019"-diameter beading wire
Quick-drying glue
2 end coils
Spring-ring clasp
Jump ring
Freshwater pearls or beads (optional)
28-gauge silver or color-coated copper wire (optional)
Size C-2 (2.75 mm) crochet hook (optional)
2 end coils (earrings)
2 earring posts (earrings)

You can make the end coils yourself. Form a spring by wrapping 22-gauge wire around one end of a knitting needle or crochet hook 10 to 20 times. Leave ¼" at the end to make an eye loop.

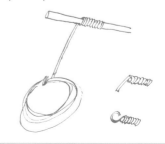

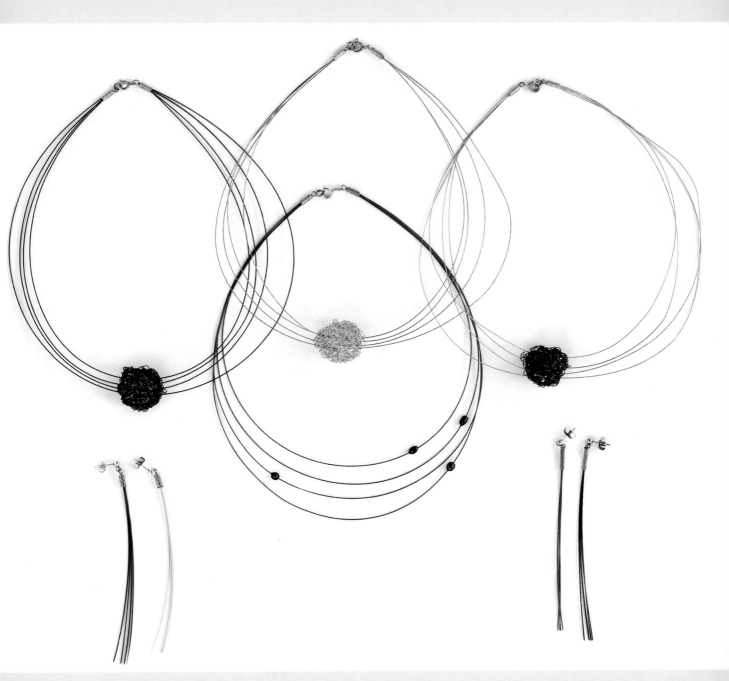

Jewelry from Lace Fragments

For these pieces of jewelry, you can use segments of small-patterned lace from an old curtain or tablecloth. Cut out small lace motifs that are so tightly structured that you can't unravel them. Machine-made lace is better for this than handmade. With some craft paint and a few small beads, the lace becomes an entirely new creation.

Cut flower motifs from lace fragments. Leave the connections between the motifs uncut. Use acrylic craft paint to paint the lace pieces gold. Test the paint first—it's better to use too little than too much. Paint a dot of red at the center of each flower. When the paint is dry, use a needle and thread or strong quick-drying glue to attach a bead to the center of each flower.

For the necklace, cut about 30 pieces of wire, 1" long. Bend each piece into links shaped in a figure eight. Shape the first loop of the figure eight by wrapping the wire around the thickest point of round-nose pliers. Make a loop in the same way on the other end of the wire, but turn the loop in the opposite direction. Embellish a few of the links with a bead at the center of the loops. The links can be tempered and flattened by carefully hammering them on a bench block. Join the links into two strands of the same length. Depending on the length you want the necklace, you may need more or fewer links. Attach each end of the lace to a chain. Attach the clasp to the other ends of the chains.

For each earring, use only one or two lace flowers. Attach it to an earring post with a jump ring. You can leave the back of the lace white or paint it with a subtle color. Glue or sew on beads.

Materials:
Lace fragments
Gold and red acrylic craft paint
Small beads
Needle and thread or glue suitable for textiles and beads
35" to 40" of 24-gauge gold-colored wire (necklace)
Toggle clasp (necklace)
2 jump rings (earrings)
2 earring posts (earrings)

Old Lace Bracelet

$\mathcal{I}$ found a long lace strip that had been lying in a drawer for years. $\mathcal{E}$ventually it became the inspiration for this bracelet. $\mathcal{M}$aybe you found some lace at a flea market or on some old linens, or you received some from a handcraft-loving relative. $\mathcal{I}$f you don't have any such small treasures, you can buy some, of course. $\mathcal{T}$ransform the lace into a special and personal piece by sewing on beads and embellishing with a pin.

Materials:
Lace strip, approximately
   2¼" x 6¾"
Cameo pin
Assorted beads
28" of narrow satin ribbon
Hand-sewing needle and
   thread
Black tea bag (optional)

Originally the lace was white, but I tinted it by dipping it in tea. Brew the tea and submerge the lace until the lace is the desired shade. Rinse, dry the lace between two towels, and steam press. Fold the raw edges under and sew to finish the edges.

Now the fun begins. Decide how romantic you want the bracelet to look. I decorated with a cameo and some shiny beads. Sew the embellishments with small invisible stitches. If there are suitable holes along the edges of the lace, you can thread a thin satin ribbon through the holes and use the ribbon to tie on the bracelet. If the holes aren't large enough to thread the satin ribbon, you can attach it to the ends (see illustration).

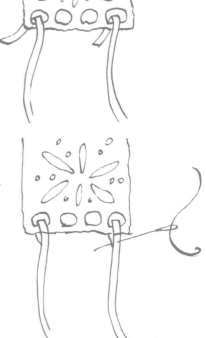

Felt and Denim Brooches

Hearts are a rewarding shape to work with, and I often return to that form for various creative projects. A heart brooch is a perfect gift for a good friend. You can make hearts in a variety of materials—denim, cotton, silk, felt, lace, leather, soft plastic—the possibilities are endless. I've made two hearts here, one with felt and the other with denim.

Felt is an easy fabric to work with because the edges won't unravel. Denim tends to unravel, but that gives a fun effect. If you don't like that look, zigzag stitch around each heart using either matching or contrasting thread.

Draw a heart shape or trace one of the hearts on this page on a piece of paper and cut it out. Lay the paper heart over the fabric and cut around it. Cut five hearts, making each succeeding heart 1/8" larger than the last. Stack the hearts and join them by sewing together with small stitches down the center of the pieces. My denim hearts are joined at the center with a star pattern stitched on the sewing machine. Finish by sewing a pin-back to the wrong side.

Materials:
Felt and denim fabric remnants
1 ½" pin-back
Hand-sewing needle and thread
Sewing machine (optional)

Felt Wrist Warmers

Wool sweaters that have seen better days can be felted to make fabric perfect for wrist warmers. For best results, use 100% wool that is not white. After felting, cut the fabric to the desired length and embellish it with beads, embroidery, or a crocheted motif.

If you don't have old jackets or sweaters to "donate," substitute felt. It won't unravel, it holds its shape, and it's very warm.

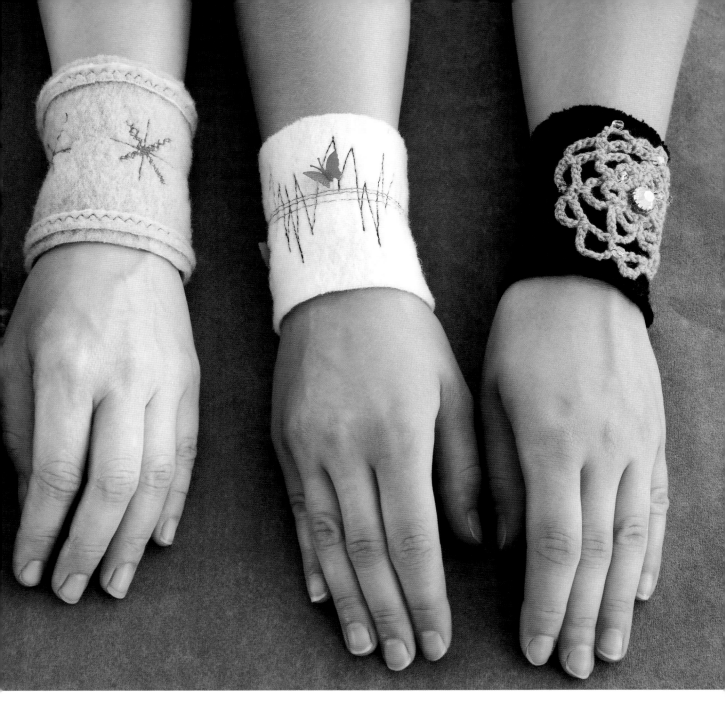

Felt the sweater by washing in a top-loading washing machine with hot water. Machine dry. Cut two rectangles, about 3¾" x 7½". The length depends on the size of your wrist. Make sure there is at least ⅜" to ⅝" of extra length for the Velcro fastener to overlap.

Embellish the fabric with your own design sewn on by hand or machine. Play around with buttons, beads, fleece, embroidery, and crocheted motifs. Use whatever you fancy!

Sew the Velcro tape to each end of the wrist warmer.

Materials:
Old sweater or felt
3¾" of ⅝"-wide Velcro tape
Hand-sewing needle and thread
Assorted buttons, beads, fleece, and so on
Sewing machine (optional)

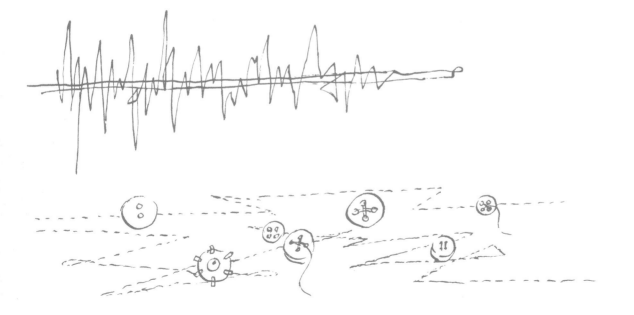

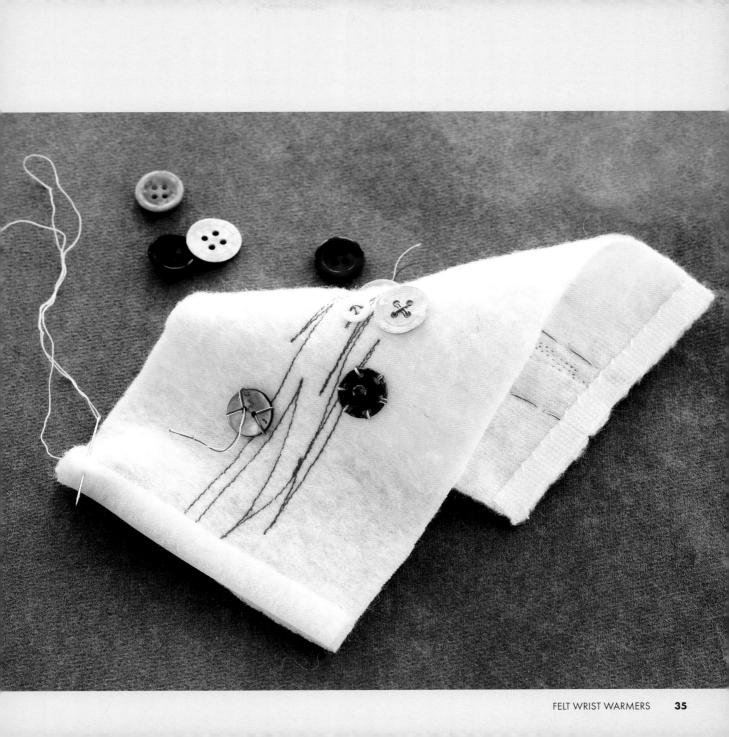

Silk Jewelry

If you have some brightly colored fabric strips and a sewing machine, you can make these lovely necklaces. As soon as you start sewing, you'll be tempted to make several pieces at the same time. Make them in various colors and patterns of fabric so you'll have necklaces for several outfits and occasions. They also make great presents.

Materials:
Lightweight silk or satin fabric
Hand-sewing needle and thread
Eye pins
3 to 4 head pins
Assorted beads and pendants
Fishhook clasp (green necklace)
4 short silver chains (green necklace)
Liver of Sulfur (green necklace)
Four 5 mm jump rings (green necklace)
Sewing machine

For the deep rose or gold necklace, cut a 2½" x 18¾" strip of fabric. Turn under ⅝" along all four edges. Fold in half lengthwise so the piece measures ⅝" x 17½". Press. Sew close to the edge with either matching or contrasting thread. Turn under 1¼" on one end of the necklace and stitch the edge to form a loop. The finished necklace measures ⅝" x 16½". For a longer necklace, start with a 2½" x 20" fabric strip.

Use the eye pins and head pins to string a selection of beads and make at least three dangles. Hang a larger pendant on the longest dangle. On the plain end of the necklace, create a small loop with doubled sewing thread and attach the bead dangles to it.

The green necklace is made in a slightly different way. Instead of a loop, it has a fishhook clasp. Begin with a 2½" x 15" rectangle of fabric. Turn under the edges, press, and sew as for the first necklace. The finished necklace measures ⅝" x 13½".

Dip the silver chain in Liver of Sulfur to darken it. Sew a 5 mm jump ring to each end of the fabric strip. Attach two more jump rings on each side. Add the clasp at one end so it can catch the rings on the other side. From each side, hang two thin chains with beads at the ends.

Beaded Silk Bands

Cut long strips of raw silk, or use silk ribbon, and decorate with freshwater pearls and glass beads. You can vary the way you wear it by wrapping the silk several times around your neck or wrist or by wearing it as a lariat, long pendant, or belt.

Necklace

Cut a 1" x 50" strip of silk fabric or 50" of ¼"-wide silk ribbon. If using the fabric, fold all four edges under ¼". Fold in half lengthwise so the strip is ¼" wide. Press and sew close to the open edges.

You can space the beads closely or sparsely. My example has about 2½" between each bead. Use round-nose pliers to form a small hook on one end of the wire, and poke this through the fabric. Form a loop and wrap it a few times to secure. Thread a bead on the wire and cut, leaving enough for a wrapped loop. Make a loop below the bead, wrap the wire a few times, and trim the excess. Attach a crystal pendant to each end of the silk.

Materials:
Lightweight silk or ¼"-wide silk ribbon
Approximately 25 glass or freshwater-pearl beads
24-gauge silver wire
2 small crystal pendants
Sewing machine

Bracelet

Cut a 20" piece of ribbon or silk. Make it the same way as the necklace. For the bracelet shown, the beads are placed in a 4" center section with ¼" between each bead. Wrap the bracelet twice around the wrist and tie.

Pretty Hearts

Copper wire is available in many thicknesses and in a wide range of colors. Start with 28-gauge wire because it's easier to shape than 24-gauge. You can choose gold, silver, red, turquoise, green, and so on. A red copper heart as a gift is symbolic and heartwarming. It's easy to make and will certainly be cherished by the recipient.

Heart

Wrap 28-gauge copper wire into a tangle, starting with an oval shape. Make another oval the same size without cutting the wire. Continue to wind the wire, joining the two pieces and using your fingers to shape the heart. When the heart is the size and shape you want, cut the wire and tuck the end into the heart.

Jewelry

For the necklace, thread the silver wire through the heart and make a small loop at each end. Bend the wire so that it will curve smoothly around the neck. Tie one end of the leather cord to one wire loop and thread it through the other. Tie two pony beads (or simply tie a knot) at the free end of the cord.

For each earring, form a small heart, ⅝" x ⅝", with 28-gauge copper wire. Attach an earring wire to a beading hoop. Thread the hoop through the center of the heart. To keep the heart upright on the hoop, put a drop of glue on the hoop before you place the heart.

For the pin, use 24-gauge copper wire to make a bolder statement. When the heart is shaped, wire it to the pin-back.

Materials:

28-gauge color-coated copper wire (necklace, earrings)

24-gauge color-coated copper wire (pin)

8" of 18-gauge silver wire (necklace)

20" of thin leather cord (necklace)

2 pony beads (necklace, optional)

2 French earring wires (earrings)

Two 20 mm beading hoops (earrings)

Quick-drying glue (earrings)

Pin-back (pin)

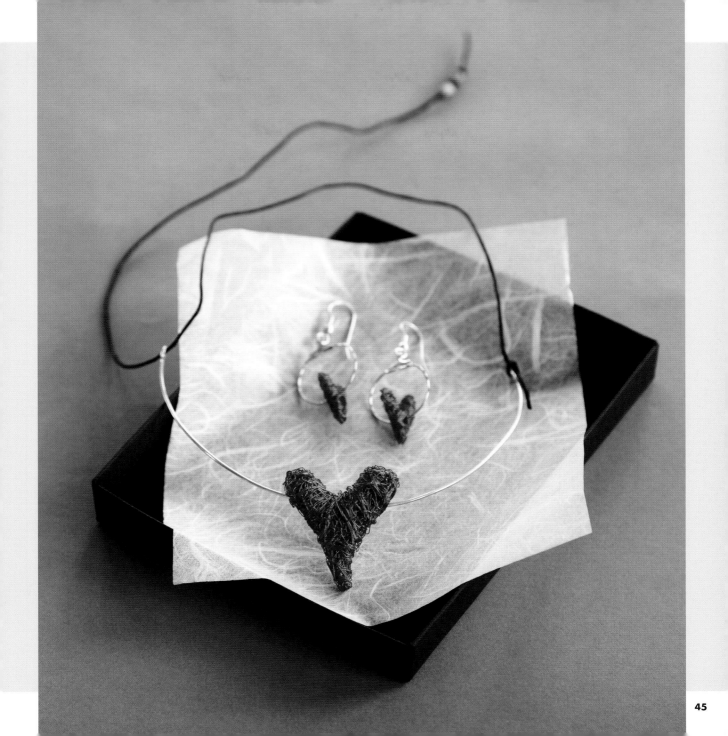

Jewelry with Wrapped Beach Glass

For this necklace, I used various lengths of thin silver chain from broken pieces of jewelry. The piece will be even more interesting if you use different thicknesses of chain. Both matt and shiny beach glass in the colors of the sea make the necklace glisten.

Necklace

Lay out the chains, glass, and beads to determine the length of the necklace. Wrap the glass pieces with wire, forming a loop on one or both ends.

Use jump rings to join the pieces and chains, placing a clasp and a large jump ring on the ends of the necklace. At the center front, hang a chain with two large glass pieces and several short chains.

Materials:
Chains of various thicknesses
    and lengths (necklace,
    earrings)
Pieces of beach glass
Glass beads (necklace,
    earrings)
24- or 28-gauge silver wire
Jump rings (necklace, earrings)
Lobster-claw clasp (necklace)
Quick-drying glue (earrings, ring)
2 French earring wires (earrings)
Flat-topped ring (ring)

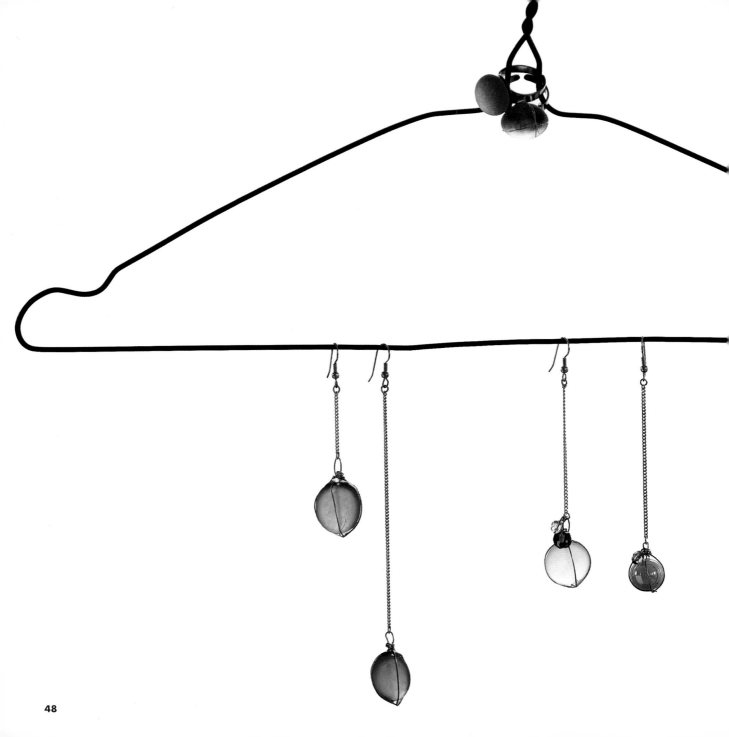

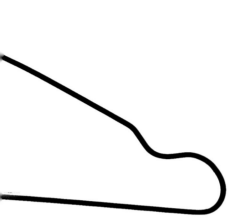

Earrings

For each earring, wrap a piece of beach glass with wire on the sides and center, and finish by making a loop. Glue at the top and bottom to secure. Use jump rings to attach the glass to a chain and earring wire. It's fun to mismatch a pair of earrings by using different shapes of glass and lengths of chain.

Ring

Rings are easy to make. Glue a piece of beach glass to the plate on a flat-topped ring. When it is dry, twist a 28-gauge wire around the glass and fasten it to the ring plate.

Birch Bark Brooch and Earrings

Nature is an infinite source of inspiration. Trees have a beautiful structure and shape, and birch trees are especially exciting because they have so many shades of color in their bark. Only use bark from firewood or stumps—the trees in the forest need to keep their bark! Birch bark can be used decoratively in a number of ways, and it makes lovely brooches, earrings, and other pieces of jewelry. Whether you have a large or small piece of birch bark, press it for a couple of days to flatten.

Brooch

Using the two large patterns on this page, cut six petals from birch bark. Use a heavy needle to make a hole on the wide end of each petal. Align the holes and form the petals into a flower. Glue the bases of the petals together. Use beading thread to tie the pin-back to the flower. Glue to secure. Attach the rhinestone or crystal flower by threading through the petal holes, tying tightly to the pin-back, and gluing to secure. As an alternative to a premade flower, you can make a little flower with small beads strung on a thread.

Secure one or two lengths of wire to the front of the brooch by poking small holes through the birch bark, threading the wire through a hole, and then twisting the end of the wire around a bead. Thread various crystals or beads on the wires.

Earrings

For each earring, use the small patterns on this page and cut three birch-bark leaves. Punch a hole at the top of each leaf with a heavy needle. Attach a jump ring through each hole. Hang a different length of chain from each earring loop and attach each leaf to a chain. Use head pins to attach small crystal dangles to two of the chains. Attach an earring wire to the hoop.

Materials:

Birch bark
Heavy needle
Quick-drying glue (brooch)
Rhinestone or Swarovski crystal flower or several beads (brooch)
Pin-back (brooch)
Beading thread (brooch)
Assorted crystals or beads (brooch)
26-gauge silver or copper wire (brooch)
Jump rings (earrings)
Assorted lengths of chain (earrings)
2 multiple-loop 30 mm earring hoops (earrings)
4 head pins (earrings)
2 French earring wires (earrings)

Decoupage Jewelry

It's fun to experiment with decoupage methods on boxes, tins, tables, and so on. You can also use the technique to make charms and beads for jewelry. Napkin motifs glued onto Styrofoam balls are quite nice. You can make balls with your own pretty and unique designs; for example, create a necklace with a few simple balls or a whole strand of them.

Materials:

Decorative paper napkins
Decoupage glue/lacquer
Paintbrush
¾" Styrofoam ball (necklace)
24-gauge wire
2 large jump rings (necklace)
18" of rattail (2 mm) satin cord (necklace)
2 crimp ends with eyes (necklace)
Spring-ring clasp (necklace)
Assorted crystals and beads
2 Styrofoam balls, ⅜" (earrings)
4 decorative bead caps (earrings)
2 French earring wires (earrings)
Quick-drying glue

Necklace

Cut motifs from a napkin. To avoid too many folds on the ball, cut the motifs into several pieces. Poke a wire through the ball and make a loop on both ends. Spread decoupage glue over the Styrofoam ball with the paintbrush. Firmly press the napkin motifs on the ball and cover them with another layer of decoupage glue. Hang the ball on a cord or small rod until it is completely dry. Glue and let dry a total of three times.

Attach a jump ring, large enough that the satin cord can easily slide through, to the ball. Dip the ends of the cord in quick-drying glue, push into the crimp ends, and crimp to secure. Add the clasp to one end of the cord and the remaining jump ring to the other end. Thread beads onto the wire and form loops on each end. Hook the beads together, making three dangles to hang under the decoupage bead.

Earrings

For each earring, use the same decoupage technique as for the necklace, except wait to thread the ball onto the wire until the last coat of glue has dried. Add the decorative bead caps before bending the wire into loops at both sides of the ball. Add another bead before attaching to the earring wire.

Crocheted Chain Necklace with Tangled-Wire Earrings

This necklace was inspired by
Dad's fishing line, which is re-created
with crocheted chains of red copper wire.
Gleaming herrings are represented by
beautiful chunks of quartz crystal.
Simple chain stitches create a chic and
noticeable piece of jewelry. Vary the
look by using other colors of
wire and different beads
and stones.

Necklace

Strand one to two crystals on the 28-gauge wire before you start crocheting. Crochet the wire into long lengths with chain stitch. When you want to place a crystal, slide it up the wire to the working chain, and then chain a stitch, catching the bead. Use the wire tails to make a small wrapped loop at each end of the chain.

Crochet 12 chains, varying the lengths from 18" to 22". Hold one end of all the chains together. With 20-gauge wire, make a ¼" hook and attach the ends of the chains. Pull the wire through an end cone and make a loop. Repeat at the other end.

Finish by attaching the clasp on one side and several jump rings on the other so that you can vary the length as desired.

Earrings

For each earring, wrap 28-gauge wire into a ball. Pull the wire through the ball several times to secure it. Shape the ball with your fingers, holding onto the end of the wire. Decide how far you want the ball to dangle, and then securely attach the wire to the earring post.

Materials:

14 to 18 drilled quartz-crystal pebbles and chips (necklace)
28-gauge copper wire (necklace, earrings)
20-gauge copper wire (necklace)
Size E-4 (3.5 mm) crochet hook (necklace)
2 end cones (necklace)
1 spring-ring clasp (necklace)
Jump rings (necklace)
2 earring posts (earrings)

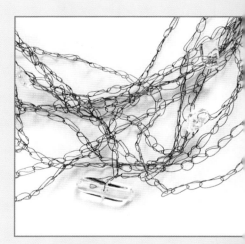

Crocheted Copper Necklace, Bracelet, and Ring

If you can crochet with yarn, you can crochet with wire, though the wire is stiffer to work with. For this necklace, I've stranded two wires together. This makes a firm necklace, but two wires are more difficult to crochet than one. If you find two wires hard to work, use one strand of 24- or 28-gauge wire and an E-4 (3.5 mm) crochet hook. Begin by making a 10-stitch x 4-row swatch to determine the number of wires and the gauge of your stitches.

Necklace

String the beads onto the 28-gauge wire. I used 38 beads, including small seed beads, nonglossy freshwater pearls, and shiny glass beads in a variety of sizes. Using the H-8 crochet hook and holding the 28-gauge wire and one strand of 24-gauge wire together, loosely crochet a chain about 24" long. Turn and single crochet back. Single crochet six to seven rows, increasing one to two stitches in each row until the piece is about 1" wide. The inside edge of the necklace should measure about 21", and the outer edge about 23". Place the beads as desired while crocheting. At some spots, pull the wire with the bead out about 3/8" and twist the wire into a "stem" so that the bead stands out for a two-dimensional appearance.

If you need to reinforce the ends, you can "sew" an extra row with copper wire at both ends. After completing the crochet, finish the necklace by attaching a chain of jump rings and small beads on one end and a clasp at the other end.

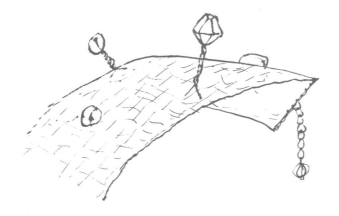

Materials:
28-gauge red copper wire (necklace, ring)
24-gauge brownish red copper wire (ring)
Assortment of red beads
Size H-8 (5 mm) crochet hook (necklace)
Size G-6 (4 mm) crochet hook (bracelet, ring)
Jump rings (necklace, bracelet)
2 lobster-claw clasps (necklace, bracelet)

Bracelet

Use the G-6 crochet hook and one strand of the 24-gauge wire. Measure your wrist to determine how long to make the bracelet. Add a few extra stitches because the piece will draw in a bit, and crochet a chain that length. Turn and single crochet rows until it is about 1½" wide. Add beads as for the necklace, or after the bracelet is crocheted, "sew" them on using the end of the wire. Attach a clasp on one end and a chain of jump rings on the other.

Ring

Use the G-6 hook and one strand of 24- or 28-gauge wire. Measure your finger and chain enough stitches to go around it. Join the chain into a ring with a single crochet stitch. Work a couple of rounds in a tight single crochet until the ring is ⅜" wide. Use the tail of the wire to fasten on the crocheted flower or star.

For the crocheted flower base, chain three and then work two rows of single crochet. Tie off. For a petal, chain five and attach to the flower base. Make five petals. Shape the petals into a flower or star. After you've finished crocheting the flower or star, attach one or several beads to the center.

Bead-Embellished Silver Plate with Leather Cord

There are many possibilities for crocheting jewelry with wire. You follow the same basic principles in each case but create new looks by varying the colors, shape, and embellishments. For this necklace, I crocheted a rectangular plate and decorated it with an assortment of beads. The piece hangs on a suede leather cord. You can use the plate for a necklace, bracelet, or brooch.

Necklace

With 24-gauge wire and the crochet hook, make a chain the desired length. This example is 2½" long. Make the long side first and single crochet back. Continue until the piece is 1¼" x 2½". The number of rows will depend on how tightly or loosely you crochet. Leave long tails of wire at the beginning and end of the crochet and use them to attach the beads. Thread beads one at a time and weave the wire through the plate to secure each bead. Spread the beads as thinly or thickly as you like. If you run out of the tail wire, twist in a new length. Finish by using pliers to firmly press the wire end under the plate so it won't scratch or loosen.

Round-nose pliers are handy for making the somewhat large holes at the top edges of the plate. Gently bore the hole with one of the jaws of the pliers. Thread the leather cord through the holes. Finish the ends of the cord with cord caps or coils and a clasp.

Attach a jump ring to the center of the bottom edge of the plate. Thread a bead on the 24-gauge wire, form a loop on each end, and attach it to the jump ring. Finish with a silver pendant.

Materials:

24-gauge silver wire (necklace, brooch, bracelets)
28-gauge silver wire (ring, bracelets)
Size 7 (4.5 mm) crochet hook (necklace, brooch)
Assorted beads
22" suede leather cord (necklace)
2 cord caps or coils (necklace)
Spring-ring clasp (necklace, bracelets)
Jump rings (necklace, bracelets)
Silver pendant (necklace)
Pin-back (brooch)

Brooch

The same plate can also be used for a brooch. Instead of the leather cord, simply attach a pin-back on the wrong side.

Ring

Crochet a ring using the 28-gauge wire. Begin with 18 firm chain stitches. Join the chain into a ring with a single crochet stitch, and work in single crochet until the ring is the desired width (for example, four rows). Use the end of the wire to sew three to five beads at the center of the ring. Using pliers, bend the wire and press it into the ring.

Bracelets

For a narrow bracelet, chain a 15" length using the wire of your choice. Before you begin the chain, thread beads onto the wire in the desired order. Place a bead on every other chain. Bend the wire ends into a loop at each side. Fold the chain in half and attach the clasp and a jump ring. This design can also be used as a simple thin necklace.

For a wide bracelet, use the bracelet instructions on page 62. Before you start crocheting, thread the beads onto the wire. Occasionally make a "stem" to stand out on the bracelet by pulling up a ⅜" length of beaded wire. Place a bead, and then twist the wire below the bead before you bring it back into the crochet work.

Silver Wire and Sewing Thread

What makes this bracelet and necklace special is the combination of silver wire and sewing thread, which gives unusual character and finish. Simply hold the wire and thread together and use a crochet hook to make the chains. Use from one to three different colors of sewing thread for the chains and add some crocheted flowers with beads.

If you want beads on your piece of jewelry, thread them onto the wire before you begin. Twist the thread a few times around the wire and make a loop at the end. Space the beads apart as you crochet the chains, about five to six beads per length.

For the necklace, crochet three separate chains with three different colors of thread. The chains should measure 14¼", 14½", and 15½". Arrange the finished lengths according to size and pull the loops through an end cap. Secure with the clasp on one end and several jump rings on the other.

Materials:
28-gauge silver wire
Sewing thread in assorted
  colors
Assorted beads
Size H-8 (5 mm) crochet hook
2 end caps
Fishhook clasp
Jump rings

Crochet a flower for the center of the piece. Hold the wire and thread together, chain three, and join into a ring with a slip stitch. Work two rounds with single crochet. Chain five, secure to the ring base with a single crochet, and chain five more. Repeat all the way around until there are five flower petals. Use the tail of the wire to attach a few beads at the center of the flower, and then attach the flower to the necklace.

For the bracelet, use the same method but crochet the strands the same length. The bracelet should measure 6¾" around the wrist. Instead of making a flower, pinch the petals into a star.

Leather Jewelry with Felted Balls

This necklace combines a few of my favorite elements: willow, felted balls, suede leather cord, and an assortment of stone chips. Sometimes you want to create a piece that has everything you like on it, but you don't know what looks best together. One suggestion is to put the pieces in a bowl, let your idea develop, and then draw out the items you think might work together. Keep trying new ideas until you come up with something you like. Suddenly your concept will become clear and you can proceed.

Necklaces

Felted balls are easy to make. Tear off a piece of merino wool roving. Mix one part wool-washing soap and two parts warm water. Dip the wool into the soapy water and squeeze out the excess. Roll the wool in the palm of your hand and rinse it with cold water. Repeat the dipping into soapy water, rolling and rinsing until the ball is the size and firmness you want. Poke a heavy needle into the ball to make a hole. Let the ball completely dry. Thread the wire through the hole and make a loop on each end.

Glue the willow sprig into the cord coil.

For the long necklace, cut 9" of light pink and 24" of green suede leather cord. Glue a cord tip at each end of the cord, and then add some jump rings. Attach the felted balls, stone chips, willow sprig, and heart and butterfly shapes to the jump rings.

For the short necklace, cut 9" lengths of both the light pink and green cords. Add embellishments as above. The length of the necklace with the dangles is 31". Attach a large spring-ring clasp to the ends of the pink cord.

Bracelet

Make the bracelet using some objects that are different from the necklace. Use jump rings instead of leather cord between the decorative items.

Materials:

Pink, white, and green merino wool roving for felted balls
Heavy needle
24-gauge silver wire
Pussy willow sprig
Suede leather cord in light pink and green (necklaces)
1 cord coil with loop
8 cord tips with loops (4 per necklace)
Jump rings
Drilled stone chips
Heart shape cut from birch bark
Butterfly shape cut from felt
Large spring-ring clasp (short necklace)
Small spring-ring clasp (bracelet)
Wool-washing soap

Braids-and-Feathers Lariat

I found some beautiful satin cords in several colors and bought a yard of each. Later it occurred to me that it would be nice to braid the three colors together. After a little experimentation, the result was these cheerful Native American–inspired necklaces with feathers and beads. Try it with your own favorite colors.

Lay the three cords together (it will look best if they don't all end at the same place, so offset the lengths a bit). Begin at the center of the cords and tightly wrap them five to six times with the wire. Tuck the end of the wire under the wraps. If you don't have a helper who can hold one end of the cords, secure the end with a clamp. Starting at the wire wrap, braid one side of the cords, leaving 8" to 10" unbraided at the end. Wrap the end of the braid with wire and secure as before (fig. 1).

1.

Glue a feather and the end of a cord in a cord tip, and press shut with flat-nose pliers. This actually takes some focus and concentration! Finish the other two cord ends the same way (fig. 2). Set the pieces aside to dry.

2.

At the other end of the cords, glue and press shut a cord tip. Finish by using the head pins and eye pins to attach some colorful beads. You can wrap the necklace once around your neck and tie it or let it hang at the full length with a knot at the front (fig. 3).

3.

You can also make braided bracelets with the same colorful mix.

Materials:
Three 1-yard lengths of rattail
   (2 mm) satin cord
28-gauge silver wire
Feathers
Quick-drying glue
6 cord tips
Head pins
Eye pins
Assorted beads

Cord Jewelry with Turquoise Felted Balls

It's fun to combine an assortment of elements that wouldn't normally go together. This can prove inspirational and fruitful, and can open up your creativity. If you limit the colors, you can choose a wide assortment of materials and the effect will still be unified. Try it!

Necklace

Make two sizes of felted balls (see page 74). Thread a silver wire through each ball and make a loop at each end of the wire. Hang a bead on one of the loops.

Crochet a gold flower with embroidery thread. Chain three, join in the round with a slip stitch in the first chain, and then work three rounds in single crochet. Chain seven and join to the base with single crochet. Make five petals the same way until you have a complete flower.

Twist a little tangled ball with turquoise copper wire (see page 58). Bend the wire into an eye loop at the end, wrap several times around the loop, and trim the excess wire. Pull the wire loop through the center of the gold flower and tie the linen cord to it.

Cut leaves from the plastic. Make a hole on one end with a heavy needle. Thread a bead on a head pin and slide it through the hole so the bead is on the front of the leaf. Form a wire loop on the back to tie the waxed cord to.

To make a fastening for the silk flower, poke a head pin through the center of the flower and bend it into an eye loop at the back.

When all the elements are prepared, tie them on the waxed cord, leaving space between each element. Tie the clasp on, leaving a little tail 2" to 2½" from the end. As a catch for the clasp, simply make a loop with the cord. Add two beads and then a crimp bead to finish the cord.

Earrings

For each earring, choose one or two favorite elements and attach them to an earring wire. You can make a variety of earrings to suit your mood.

Materials:
Felted balls
24-gauge silver wire
24-gauge turquoise copper wire
Assorted beads and charms
Size 7 (4.5 mm) crochet hook
Gold embroidery thread
20" of white waxed linen cord
1 mm–thick white plastic
Heavy needle
Head pins
Small silk flowers
Spring-ring clasp
Crimp bead
Earring wires (earrings)

Necklace and Bracelet with Beads and Leather Flowers

I cut flower shapes from leather remnants to make an especially lively necklace. The waxed jewelry cord is doubled and tied around the large beads. The combination of wooden and clear green glass beads contributes to the natural look.

Materials:

Leather or synthetic leather remnant
24-gauge silver wire
Green and black glass beads in various sizes
Black wooden beads
60" moss green waxed jewelry cord
Spring-ring clasp (bracelet)

Necklace

Using the patterns on this page, cut four flowers from the leather remnant. Make a hole at the center of each flower and thread with a piece of wire. Thread a glass bead on the wire on the front of each flower. Make a loop at each end of the wire.

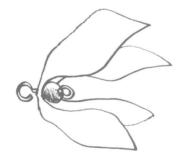

Double the waxed jewelry cord and make a 1½" loop at the center. String a large green bead on one strand of the cord and a small glass bead on the other. Knot the strands together after stringing the beads. Alternate green and black beads between the knots and place flowers approximately 4" to 5" apart. Use a small decorative bead as a stopper between the large beads. End with a leather flower and a new knot. Leave 4¼" at the end of the cords loose, and attach two small beads to the ends. To wear the necklace, simply bring one end through the cord loop.

Bracelet

Use the same technique for the bracelet, but finish with a spring-ring clasp.

Beach Combings

When you're on vacation and strolling along the beach, you can collect some lovely little treasures, including sand-ground stones and glass, shells, crab claws, snail shells, or bits of coral. You can make an exciting piece of jewelry by combining the beach combings with purchased beads. Just make sure that your beach treasures are strong enough to hold to the chain.

Necklace

Carefully drill a hole in the shells and crab claws. It's a good idea to bring a few extras from the beach, because some might break. Attach a head pin or eye pin to each of the pieces and form a loop.

Wrap the wire around the beach glass. Use the same method as for wrapping a package with ribbon. Pull the wire tightly so that it won't loosen, and twist the ends together. Form a wrapped loop with one of the wire ends.

Thread eye pins through the beads and make a loop.

String the chains and decorative pieces together, and attach a clasp and jump ring to the ends. Make a long dangle using wire, beach combings, small bits of chain, and French wire (bullion) for the center of the necklace.

Bracelet

Make a bracelet in the same way but omit the dangle.

Earrings

For each earring, drill two opposing holes in the shell. Thread a headpin through each hole, trim, and form in a loop. Use a jump ring to attach two glass beads on one end of the shell and the earring wire on the other.

Materials:
Assorted shells and crab claws
Jump rings
28-gauge silver wire (necklace, bracelet)
Beach glass (necklace, bracelet)
Eye pins (head pins)
Assorted glass beads and chips
Spring-ring clasp (necklace, bracelet)
Thin chain segments (necklace)
French wire (necklace)
French earring wires (earrings)
Small rotary drill

Asian-Inspired Jewelry

$\mathcal{I}$ combined strands of raw silk, velvet, and lining fabric for this lovely and colorful design. $\mathcal{I}$ unraveled one of the fabrics for a rough edge and then braided the strands into a thick cord. $\mathcal{A}$ good alternative is to use fabric remnants or old ribbon that has been in your stash for a while because you haven't known what to do with it.

Necklace

You can hem the fabric strips or leave some with raw edges. The width of the strips can vary from ¾" to 1½", depending on the fabric thickness. It's important that the thickness of the strips is similar. With thread, tightly wrap the three strips together at one end and secure by sewing through all the strips. Braid the strips and wrap the other end with thread as before.

Make a hook with the wire and slide it through one end of the braid. Thread a bell cap through the wire, glue the fabric ends in the bell cap, tighten it, and make an end loop. Finish the other end of the braid the same way.

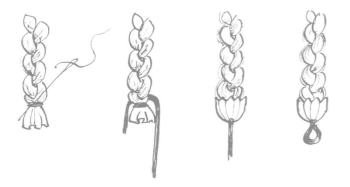

Attach the toggle clasp with the large jump ring, which will also serve as a decorative detail. The necklace's length, including the clasp, should be about 19¾".

Use a Styrofoam ball for a pendant at the front. Cut out small bits of fabric and use decoupage glue to glue them to the Styrofoam ball, completely covering it. Let the ball dry. Use the heavy needle to make a hole through the ball. Thread the wire through the ball and make a loop at both ends. Hang the ball from the toggle ring.

Hang the small jump ring from the lower loop of the ball, and then attach a curtain tassel to the jump ring.

Bracelet

Make as for the necklace, but omit the tassel and use narrower fabric strips and a spring-ring clasp.

Nostalgic Beaded Cross

Make a cross that features a miniature photo, and then add details that have special meaning for you. This cross starts with a basic wire form, which is then embellished with beads and glass flowers. A velvet ribbon completes the vintage look.

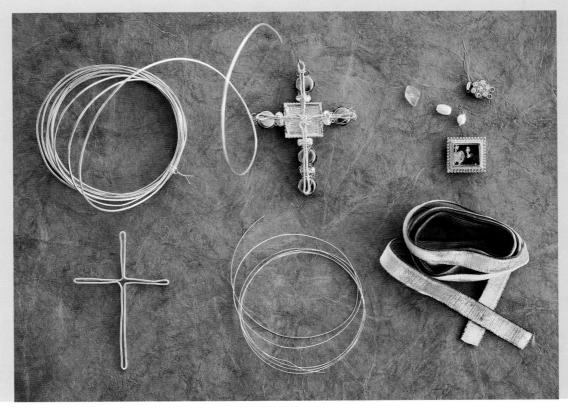

Necklace

Bend the 18-gauge wire into four flat loops to make a cross shape that is 2½" high and 2" wide. Begin and end at the center of the cross. Reinforce the center by wrapping it with 28-gauge wire. Attach the framed picture to the center. It is important that the frame has holes so you can attach it firmly with wire. Alternating the beads and flowers, use the 28-gauge wire to wind them tightly to the cross.

Materials:

18-gauge silver wire (necklace)

28-gauge silver wire (necklace)

Photographic frame or plate with holes (necklace)

Freshwater-pearl beads

Crystal or rhinestone flowers (with holes)

Jump rings (necklace)

29½"-long velvet ribbon (necklace)

13¾"-long velvet ribbon (bracelet)

Drilled quartz pebbles (bracelet)

Needle and thread (bracelet)

The metal frame for the cross should not be visible on the front except at the very top where a bit of the wire will stick out. Attach a jump ring at that end and then into the center of the 29½"-long velvet ribbon. Tie the ribbon in a bow at the back of the neck.

Bracelet

Starting at the center of the 13¾"-long velvet ribbon, sew on the beads, quartz pebbles, and flowers. Sew from the back with small stitches so the ribbon won't pucker.

Painted Russian Balls

Ethnic culture has inspired design for a very long time. Make your own Russian-inspired necklace by painting your choice of motifs on wooden balls. Choose your colors first. Fewer color combinations will be more effective, although many colors make a bolder impression and that may be exactly what you want. If the design doesn't look right to you, paint over it with the background color and begin again.

Use the medium paintbrush and acrylic paint to paint the background on the wooden balls. If you place the balls on skewers, the paint will dry more evenly. Paint the motifs on the balls with the fine brush. I used two colors: orange and a pinkish red. When the balls are dry, use the waterproof pen to outline the shapes and add details. Coat the balls with decoupage glue and let them dry.

Arrange the balls in a ring, mixing small and large ones in a nice balance of colors and size. For a long necklace, use a 43" strip of silk. For a short necklace, use a 24" strip. I left the raw edges on the fabric for a rough look. If you don't like the raw edges, use ribbon. String the balls on the silk or ribbon and make a knot before and after each ball.

You can make an adjustable-length necklace by tying it at the back of the neck. For a fixed length, attach a clasp instead.

Rose-Petal Hearts

Pressed petals and flowers are very pretty. You can collect some when you are on vacation or pick a few from your own yard or patio. Rose petals dry quickly and are easy to work with. Pick large petals with clear colors and press them between newspaper for a week. Keep them in their natural form or cut them into various shapes, such as hearts. These fragile treasures can be preserved by encasing them in plastic.

Necklace

Cut heart shapes from the rose petals and laminate them. Leave a ⅜" space between hearts so you'll have room to cut around each piece. If you don't have access to a laminating machine, use self-adhesive laminating sheets, available at office-supply stores. When you encase the rose petals in the plastic, make sure that all bubbles are smoothed out.

For a necklace, cut out each heart, leaving a ⅛" plastic border around each. Use a heavy needle to *carefully* prick a hole at the top and bottom or on each side of the heart. Laminate some extra hearts so you can practice. Form S hooks with the wire and attach them to the hearts through the holes.

Thread each bead with an eye pin and form a loop. Make sure the beads aren't too heavy or the chain will break. String the chain, beads, and hearts together, and place the clasp on one end of the necklace and the jump ring on the other.

Make a bracelet or earrings the same way as the necklace.

Materials:
Pressed rose petals
Laminating machine or self-laminating sheets
Heavy needle
24-gauge gold-colored wire
Glass or crystal beads
Rose quartz beads
Eye pins
Gold chain
Large jump ring
Lobster-claw clasp

Origami Birds and Fans

Origami is the Japanese art of folding paper. Origami paper comes in many beautiful designs. Experiment with a range of paper from thin and transparent to heavier coated papers. Coated paper is harder to fold than uncoated, but it's more durable. Start with a fan, because it's the easiest figure to make. To make the pieces more durable, lightly coat them with a thin layer of clear acrylic spray or decoupage glue.

Fan

Cut a 2½" x 4" piece of paper and accordion fold it in ¼"-wide creases. Press hard along the fold lines with your fingernail or a ruler. On the outside edge, cut the corners at a diagonal. Use a heavy needle to make a hole at the center of the fan and insert a head pin. Fold the two ends together and glue. Clamp and let dry.

For each earring, thread a small bead on the head pin before adding the fan. Glue the center folds of the fan together. Make a loop at the top of the pin and mount it on an earring wire.

If you want to make a double fan, make two fans as above, and then glue them together.

Birds

It isn't difficult to make birds once you've had some practice, but at the beginning, it can take some fiddling to fold such a small shape. Become familiar with the technique by practicing with a 6" x 6" square of inexpensive paper. For the large bird, start with a 1¾" x 1¾" square. The small bird uses a 1¼" x 1¼" square. It is very important to make the folds even and flat, with sharp points. Take the time and care to make the first folds precisely, and the results will be terrific.

1. Fold the square in half on the diagonal. Open and fold in half again on the opposite diagonal (fig. 1).
2. Fold in the outer edges, aligning them at the vertical center (fig. 2).
3. Fold up the lower flaps. These will eventually be the wings (fig. 3).
4. Open the flaps at the top of the figure and carefully pull the inner flap forward so the two pieces separate. Smooth both sections (figs. 4 and 5).
5. Turn the figure over.
6. Bring the top flap forward and the wing flaps backward, folding in half so that the two wings meet at the back, and the main flaps separate from each other (it will look like a folded triangle inside another triangle (figs. 6 and 7).
7. Fold the wing flaps up. Make a fold for the head (fig. 8). Make a hole near the base of the tail with a needle or pin.

Materials:

Paper
Heavy needle
Head pins in 3 different lengths
Quick-drying glue
Small beads
Six 20-gauge, 2¼"-long eye pins (necklace)
20-gauge copper or silver wire (necklace)
Two ¼"-diameter jump rings (necklace)
Spring-ring clasp (necklace)
French earring wires (earrings)
Acrylic spray or decoupage glue/lacquer (optional)

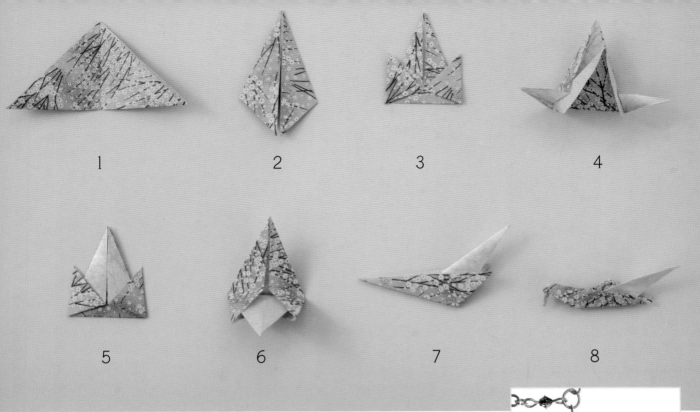

For each earring, make one large and two small birds. String a bead and then a bird on each of three head pins. Cut the head pins three different lengths. Use round-nose pliers to form a loop on the end of each head pin. Attach three birds to each earring wire.

For a necklace (see the photo at right and on page 108), make one large and two small birds, each from a different color. Use the eye pins to make the chain. Make a loop at the straight end of each pin. Use the wire to make six S hooks with a bead at each center. Join the eye pins and S hooks to a jump ring at the center and a clasp at the ends.

Attach three different lengths of head pins to the birds, and attach them to the jump ring. You can vary the design by adding a glass bead before attaching the bird, creating a flying "bird with an egg."

More Great Jewelry-Making Books from Martingale & Company®

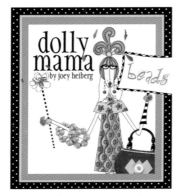

Dolly Mama Beads

by Joey Heiberg

80 pages, full-color

The Beader's Handbook

by Juju Vail

256 pages, full-color

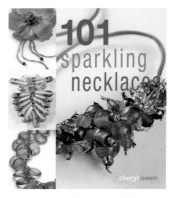

101 Sparkling Necklaces

by Cheryl Owen

128 pages, full-color

**Friendship Bracelets
All Grown Up**

by Jo Packham

64 pages, full-color

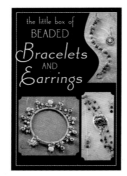

**The Little Box of Beaded
Necklaces and Earrings**

20 full-color
laminated project cards

**The Little Box of Beaded
Bracelets and Earrings**

20 full-color
laminated project cards

1-800-426-3126

International: 1-425-483-3313 • **Fax:** 1-425-486-7596 • **Email:** info@martingale-pub.com